T0208710

POLITICAL IDEOLOGY
AND
STATESMANSHIP
DURING
TIMES OF TURMOIL

POLITICAL IDEOLOGY AND STATESMANSHIP DURING TIMES OF TURMOIL

PROFESSOR WANDA FUSTER, MS. ECONOMICS

WESTBOW
PRESS®
A DIVISION OF THOMAS NELSON
& ZONDERVAN

WestBow Press books may be ordered through booksellers or by contacting:

WestBow Press
A Division of Thomas Nelson & Zondervan
1663 Liberty Drive
Bloomington, IN 47403
www.westbowpress.com
1 (866) 928-1240

Scripture quotations are taken from The Holy Bible, New International Version®, NIV® Copyright © 1973, 1978, 1984, 2011 by Biblica, Inc.® Used by permission. All rights reserved worldwide.

This book is a work of non-fiction. Unless otherwise noted, the author and the publisher make no explicit guarantees as to the accuracy of the information contained in this book and in some cases, names of people and places have been altered to protect their privacy.

ISBN: 978-1-9736-5389-9 (sc)

Library of Congress Control Number: 2019901879

Print information available on the last page.

WestBow Press rev. date: 07/17/2019

CONTENTS

CONTENTS

DEDICATION

To my Parents Ana and Roberto and to my beloved husband George for all of their love and support along my career and life.

PREFACE

This Book is an attempt to share my preoccupations in terms of our country (United States) Public policy. Every single politician should be called to work with an intricate great amount of public policies and to hold decisions on what is better or wrong. I did the analysis between what to say about what was good or what was bad for my understanding of these policies. However is not a completed mission, when we avoid doing what we have to do because the fears of been criticized are coming to our minds. I do make my own critical analysis of what was wrong or what was good for the public policies between the decade of the 60's, 70's and 80's. This is my first volume and I'm looking forward to more after the 80's until our times of turmoil. As an American Citizen, my intentions are to be a help and to contribute to our society with a group of important facts but been looking through the lenses of the sovereign Government of God, because inside the intentions of the politicians between these decades was to keeping the clear desire to please their constituency no matter that for many other people these policies were unfair on the sense of their high financial cost to our nation. Meanwhile, I was starting my studies of Ph.D. I went totally in love with this subject of public policy.

CHAPTER 1

WORLDVIEW AND POLITICAL IDEOLOGY

During the 60's, 70's and the 80's, there was an establishment of public policies that generated changes in the wellbeing of the poor and minorities. Race and poverty were the epicenter of these so-called reforms or public policies that President Kennedy was trying to implement due to its mandate in the 60's, and continued after Kennedy's passing through President Johnson, President Nixon, President Carter and President Reagan. The welfare programs were for the preservation of the family unit. With that being said there was great dissatisfaction with the welfare system management because some sectors of the government believed that was a negative precedent the prevalence of the long term welfare aid. The government found a lot of corruption, pointing on the widows and their small children recipients of the AFDC welfare program. Many of these women were not officially widows, with some were having babies each single year. Something that bothered the different levels of government officers was the lack of moral values of the welfare recipients during those days. In America, having children in the sanctity of the marriage was the standard of living and the alternative lifestyles were not accepted at that time. There was a lot of resentment from the poor communities that were submitted to the affluent people's conservative standards. But the policies were a big step to support to try to push the poor population to have an incentive to get out from their poverty. In the further paragraphs, I will discuss every one of the implemented policies that were established during the 1960s until the 1980s.

The first policy is the AFDC-Aid to Families with Dependent Children. This program was intended to help widows and their children. What was wrong with this policy is that the affluent policymakers were tired of finding continued use of the welfare funds and programs to sustain poor families with many more children than the affluent families, without been submitted to some sort of life ethics — like the covenant mandate of the sanctity of marriage. Another possibility was that some welfare recipients were having three, four, or five children with different fathers. Their life values were weaker than many affluent families who were trying to have children inside wedlock.

What is wrong with this public policy is that this problem represents a moral hazard. When the government implements a policy to sustain somebody with a program or finances, the government should know that these people understand that they should be in good, moral behavior. This wasn't the case during the 60s among the poor population in United States. The problem is the moral decay of America's people. What is right about this policy was the intention to protect the minors by offering their moms the necessary resources to feed them well.

The food stamp program was created to provide food, essentially feeding the poor families and their children with better quality food, and to make sure their children were properly fed. What is right about this policy is the intention to provide food to give the children and their parents the essentials to survive, which matches with the "justice for all" that we have from our covenantal agreement with the Lord God's natural laws. That policy helps the people to keep the freedom established in that covenant, because they are not in need of stealing food from a market or somebody else's home.

Medicare was created to provide the poor with health insurance in their old age, to the families with medical care, to support and help those live better lives and to protect their right of life that also is established in our covenantal laws of God.

Public housing was created for the purpose of giving the poor a place to live and to be able to have a secure place for their children. This policy is right because it helps people to maintain a house or a secure place in which they can feel that they have some sort of property rights, which is an inalienable right.

The Manpower training was an opportunity for many other people to be able to select their career path and to pursue some level of economic independence through having a better job. What is right from that policy is that it promotes economic development and helps to preserve their right to liberty, avoiding the need to steal or make wrong decisions that could harm their futures.

The social welfare was another policy created with the intention to sustain the poor people financially. This policy again helps to sustain economically these individuals and make them more independent until they can get out from the pervasive poverty situation. What is wrong with this policy is that it could be perpetuating their economic dependence on the government.

The anti-poverty bill was created to inspire the human responses to be able to get out from the culture of poverty, but it was a necessity to prove the successful outcomes in front of the government authorities and the programs should be able to removing people from the welfare rolls. What is wrong with this policy is that the outcomes sometimes weren't as expected because people were more inclined to rely on some type of continuous economic support.

Loan programs and community development programs were training programs. Community action programs helped develop the depressed neighborhoods and entire communities to bring the people opportunities to escape from welfare dependency. What was wrong with these policies? The federal Government was leading a movement to restrict and limit the use of welfare. There has probably been a hypocritical management of these policies with the sole purpose of getting political candidates to bring their constituents to the polls in cities. The politicians need people, diversity, and followers. After the people are recipients of welfare, it's more common to see militancy on the part of parties and minority groups.

The demands of the poor people's campaign was for an "economic bill of rights," that guaranteed all citizens a job or income. The poor people's campaign made these six demands: an end to hunger, an end to bad housing, an end to unemployment and guaranteed incomes for those unable to work, adequate health care for all citizens, full equality of educational opportunity for all, and the end of violence and repression at home and abroad.

▮ Evaluation of the major Political Ideologies influencing the policy arena

The two major political ideologies influencing the policy arena are the Republican and the Democrat. Both ideologies are coming from beliefs about diversity on political, social, and religious points of view. The Supreme Court of the United States sided with the constitutional rights of individuals. That was the beginning of the Open Society, whose values were running counter to moral values of groups on both the left and the right of the political spectrum.

Since 1890, there were the conventions of the People's Party. The People's Party was a populist tradition from the marginalized masses, unskilled workers and small farmers that seemed threatened by the development of modernization. They were the "new right" that were very different from the Old Republican conservatives. The Old Republicans were very rich, professionals who were well educated. Some of them were the owners of the big business elite. There was a revolution against secularization to increase the social permissiveness of the culture in the United

States. The New Right was fighting against the Open Society, in which the secular views were used to apply new policies, like the policy created following the Supreme Court case Roe vs. Wade that creates the right to make an abortion legal. Certain other ideas like the queer theory, feminism, Marxism, the critical theory, multiculturalism, liberalism, conservatism, and liberal Socialism, among others, would be discussed.

Queer Theory

This theory was influenced by the work of Lauren Berlant, Leo Bersani, Judith Butler, Lee Edelman, Jack Halberstam, and Eve Kosofsky Sedgwick. Queer theory builds both upon feminist challenges to the idea that gender is part of the essential self and upon gay/lesbian studies' close examination of the socially constructed nature of sexual acts and identities. Whereas gay/lesbian studies focused its inquiries into natural and unnatural behavior with respect to homosexual behavior, queer theory expands its focus to encompass any kind of sexual activity or identity that falls into normative and deviant categories. This theory is supported by some part of the feminist social movement.

What is wrong with this theory is the fact that it is against the clear categories – man and woman -- created by the Lord. No other categories or new identities created or implemented by society should be accepted. It's only the identities of God's creation and the mandate to form the family base when he declares in the Bible: 'It is not good for the man to be alone. I will make a helper suitable for him.' Then the Lord God made a woman from the rib, he had taken out of the man, and he brought her to the man." Clearly the Lord constructed the genders of man and woman, not anything else. I reject the idea that society constructs the nature of sexual acts and identities. The only constructor of natural sexual orientation is God. The only identities are the man and woman, made by the Creator God. The gospel commandments are very clear on that particular point.

■ Marxism

Marxism is a method of socio-economic analysis that views class relations and social conflict using a materialist interpretation of historical development and takes dialectical views of social transformation. It originates from the 19th century by Karl Marx and Friedrich Engels. What is wrong with this method of socio-economic analysis is its oppressive and determinant view of the people's right to liberty, life and property. Marxist Ideology attacked the political ideologies that protect those inalienable rights and Christian believers, mostly on their concepts of what is considered right and what is considered wrong. Marxism even diminishes the value of love and justice that comes from the sovereign law and will of God. I do not agree with this type of political ideology. I consider this an attack on the people's civil liberties and a movement to destroy our inalienable right to have our own properties or homes, our preservation of our own life, to participate in the free market and to be able to have our own views and liberties to practice our religion in an open way without being condemnd, jailed and tortured by the government, as happened in the times of Marxism and Leninism. God gave a powerful weapon in his covenant with his people. He gave the commandments that are our basic and most powerful natural law, to avoid the moral decay that could be jeopardizing our nation's stability.

Critical Theory

The critical theory is based on how to gain access to control others using hate speech. This is considered a part of the Marxist ideology. What is wrong with this theory is that it is against the biblical principles of the sovereign model of government and statesmanship because it uses the force of the spirit of hate toward others that are not alienated with their aggressive ways to try to control others. When a person is able to control himself, he's no longer willing to be controlled by an arbitrary tyrannical government.

▨ Multiculturalism

In the context of political philosophy, multiculturalism involves ideologies and policies ranging from the advocacy or equal respect for the various cultures in a society through policies promoting cultural diversity to policies in which people of various ethnic and religious groups are addressed by the authorities according to the group to which they belong. What is wrong with this policy is that this political philosophy allows the stronger and more financially advantaged groups to exploit and take advantage of the poorer, more disadvantaged, and vulnerable cultures or ethnic groups.

▨ Liberalism

Liberalism is the political and moral philosophy based on liberty and equality. It supports civil rights, gender equality, democracy, and racial equality, freedom of religion and freedom of speech. What is right with this ideology is the wide breadth of liberties and the many different acceptances of many types of beliefs. But what is wrong is that it is not attached to the Biblical principles of the covenantal laws of the Lord that help to keep our basic liberties grounded in clear respect for the model of the government and statesmanship of a sovereign God.

Conservatism

Conservatism is a political and social philosophy promoting traditional social institutions in the context of culture and civilization. It includes the covenantal perspective that society needs a healthy family. This philosophy is right because it's consistent with a model in which the people are submitted to the Lord God's sovereign laws through covenant.

Socialism

Socialism is the political and social philosophy in which people believe that they have to share their property, economic means are owned solely by the sole government, and personal liberties should be submitted to the government's will. What is wrong with this political philosophy of government is that it doesn't recognize the personal liberties of the people and does not allow the right to practice religious beliefs. The view is that the government should be more inclined to include what is most accepted in secular society, and to live without the covenant of God. When the supreme power is the government and the people have limited freedom of speech and limited access to a free market. Tyranny would have a good chance to develop in this type of government.

Biblical model of government and statesmanship

The Biblical model of God's government and statesmanship applied to the specific policies of Part 1 are directed by the terms of Justice for all when they are implementing the program of AFDC-Aid to families with dependent children. When the needy are asking for something, the Lord is the best provider. Concerning the policy of food provision it is best to implement the covenantal relationship as the basis for society's wellbeing. The other policies implemented -- welfare funds, food stamps, Medicare, public housing, manpower training, social welfare, anti-poverty bills, loans, community development programs, training and community programs are all the basis of the public policy to reduce poverty during the reform period. During the Johnson years, poverty was reduced from 18% to 13% from 1964 to 1968.

Covenant and Federalism

Federalism is a form of government in which there is a division of powers between two levels of government with equal status. The covenant government is formed by a covenant of the people; just government is achieved by willful concessions of power; just government is upheld by mutual obligation; just government is protected by rule by consent; just government is protected by separation of powers; just government is established by a constitution; just government can only function properly with self-government; and just government can only function properly with loving fulfillment of covenant obligations. What is right about this is that the government is based on the Lord God's sovereign and statesmanship model to pursue the inalienable rights of liberty, life and property. People should be able to have a better life when they are aligned to this model of God's sovereign government.

▨ Institutional separations of church and state/ Sin-Crime distinction

The church and state have separate functions. The church not being endorsed by the state does not mean the separation of the state from Biblical principles. Sin is recognized when man is held accountable by the Lord for its outcome. Crime is when somebody makes a wrong decision and breaks a specific type of law in the secular world. When we commit a crime the Lord makes clear that we should be accountable for that crime. God is the creator and ruler of the Universe.

▨ Resisting tyranny

The Lord God's sovereign government and statesmanship is the best type of government because it guarantees the people just treatment. Acknowledging the sovereignty of God as the basis of government enforces the need for justice in government, covenantal relationships as the basis for society, maintains a proper relationship between church and state, and prevents tyranny in government. The great thing about this covenantal provision is justice and the right to life, property, and liberty. Also important is the support for access to free markets and the free exercise of religion.

CHAPTER 2

FISCAL AND MONETARY POLICIES

■ I-The key debates in fiscal and monetary policies

■ Supply and money flow

A key debate in economic policy pertains to the way in which the government controls the supply and flow of money in the economy. The creation of monetary policy was to expand or contract the amount of money in circulation through the Federal Reserve Board. The Federal Reserve serves as the bank of banks and as the central bank of the United States, working to stabilize the economy with the creation of regulations. The first control to regulate the economy is through the money supply using the OMO-Open market operations board to purchase or sell government bonds. Buying these bonds places money directly in the hands of potential spenders. But, if they sell these bonds, they reduce the flow of money available or in circulation. Increasing the amount of money in distribution serves to stimulate demand and economic expansion, but can also lead to inflation. Decreasing the money supply reduces the requirement for products or services but pushes the inflation out that could be stimulating higher unemployment rates. Today, we are not using gold; the value of American currency is determined by the supply of money in circulation and the level of confidence in the American economy. One of the debates related to fiscal policy is the government spending tax dollars to strengthen the economy when people could have money in their hands to spend on products and services. The other leg of the monetary policy is the imposing of taxes to cut economic activity and control inflation. Also when the government reduces taxes, this encourages corporations to expand their operations and impact the employment rates positively. When the government manages the national debt, this creates controversy, but this is also another type of fiscal policy. The Republicans or conservatives in Congress are the lawmakers that believe in *laissez-faire* and do not believe in the expansion of government intervention. The conservatives are more inclined to deregulate industries and to ease the business development to stimulate the economy and the economic expansion. On the other hand, we have the Democrats or liberals that believe in more government regulations. The controversy about the types of rules or policies is going to continue because the public expectation of the government's role is to maintain an active intervention in employment creation and to maintain economic growth. People's access to the money supply Stimulation and expansion of product sales or services should be measured by the Federal government to encourage spending in case of recession or to control the impact in case of inflation. How much government intervention is enough, or acceptable? What should the role of the federal government be in achieving lower unemployment rates? On the other side, what role should it take in economic growth measured by the GDP — gross domestic product — which represents the total value of production of goods and services? Should the government be involved in determining how much is necessary to produce and for whom? Is it essential that the Federal Government play a role in promoting GDP expansion? Should the federal government play a role in economic equality? Is that something expected by the constituents? Should the government actively pursue policies that seek the redistribution of financial wealth? What level of involvement should the government have in business? Is Governmental involvement consistent with the free enterprise economic system? After a close review of these different economic values, the economic policies become the central part of the political compromises and the exercise of power by political parties. In American history, economic policies have been based on a mixture of different liberal/progressive and conservative values.

▨ Murray's claims, about the critical failings of the State

▨ The obligation to help the poor

According to Douglas Alexander, the responsibility of governments to protect and help the poor citizens of the country is not only a matter of charity but of justice. Moreover, he claims that the response to the poor is not only a matter for the government but for all citizens. He goes even further in stating that responsibility for the poor does not only affect those living in the same country, but also those living in any other part of the world. To illustrate such a claim, Alexander suggests the example of two unfortunate girls living just a few kilometers apart from each other. One of the girls lives in India, while the other lives in Bangladesh. Through this example, Alexander demonstrates how unfair it would be to any of the girls if the government were only to help one of them. In this regard, he pinpoints how responsibility to the poor does not know barriers between countries, as poverty itself is the same throughout different countries, and the fundamental needs of the two girls are identical regardless of where they live. Thus, both the girls living in India and Bangladesh need something as essential as access to potable and safe drinking water, shelter, and food to survive.

As per Murray, the government's responsibility to the poor should not marginalize either of these two girls, and any government on earth should provide for both girls' most basic needs. Even while the response to the poor would thus be a universal matter, and affect governments worldwide, Murray suggests that not one of these government interventions succeeds in helping the poor. Even while certain countries, like the United Kingdom, have implemented several programs to aid these people, these programs are generally ineffective either because they never raise enough funds to really make a difference in the lives of the millions of poor people worldwide, or they fail to reach those that really need the assistance, or they are able only to bring partial relief.

◼ 2-The change in Incentives

A second major problem in which the government of different countries tends to fail is in the necessary change in the incentives provided to companies to promote the economic growth of the country and the creation of jobs. In this sense, Murray suggests how the absence of job incentives resulted in the massive dropout from labor force, as companies did not provide people with a stable job perspective.

◼ 3-Increase dropout from the labor force

According to Murray's observation, the welfare incentives provided by the U.S. government caused the dropout from the labor force en masse. Such an increased rate in the number of employees that dropped out was especially significant among poor males from ages 16 to 24. However, while the facts were true, Murray failed to interpret them correctly. As I will explain later, this claim has been repeatedly refuted by several scholars. The reason for Murray's misinterpretation of the facts resided in the fact that he undervalued the connection existing between social welfare programs and poverty, thus resulting in a biased and hence faulty perception of how social welfare would have impacted poverty.

4-Poverty and Welfare Dependency

According to Murray, welfare incentives provided by the government would have failed to alleviate the poverty issue, but rather resulted in poor people becoming dependent on such welfare. This analysis has however been criticized on several occasions by economists and sociologists. For instance, O'Connor suggests that the fundamental problem is that government makes it affordable for women to bear and raise children without husbands, while living independently in households of their own. If a society believes that marriage is the best arrangement for the well-being of men, women, and children, then its laws and customs must reflect that belief seriously, consistently, and effectively.

High benefit levels and lax attitudes toward sex

and marriage create a world in which many children have few or no ties to their fathers, in which mothers, increasingly unmarried, are more often abused and exploited, and in which many men join gangs and take up crime as a way of life. This is a world not only of financial poverty but also of emotional chaos and physical danger. It is not Hobbes's state of nature, but life is increasingly "nasty" and "brutish".

One cannot help being reminded of Benjamin Franklin's final verdict on the British welfare system. He argued that supporting people who chose not to work promoted poverty. The contemporary outlook on welfare has both propelled the family's disintegration and encouraged vast dependence. Amending its perverse incentives and harmful effects on the family would require reforms not only in welfare law but also in family law, property regulation, and more. An analysis of these reforms exceeds the scope of this paper.

Many today fail to note that antipoverty programs can easily have a corrupting effect if they are not set up in a way that promotes rather than undermines the morality of self-restraint and self-assertion that is a necessary foundation of what Jefferson called "temperate liberty." Both Jefferson and Franklin supported laws that encourage responsibility toward family and community, self-sufficiency, and industriousness. They understood that political freedom rests on the moral character of the people.

The incentive structure of the modern welfare state is similar to the one that Franklin condemned in old England, except that ours is more generous and more tolerant of single motherhood. Since 1965, when President Lyndon Johnson inaugurated the modern "War on Poverty," total annual government welfare spending has grown from less than $9 billion(1.3 percent of gross domestic product) to $324 billion(five percent of GDP) in 1993 to $927 billion(six percent of GDP) in 2011. Between 1965 and 2013, the government spent $22 trillion (adjusted for inflation) on means-tested welfare programs—more than three times the costs of all military wars in the history of the United States.

Evaluating Welfare Spending with a Biblical Model of Government and Statesmanship

The Biblical principles of government and statesmanship argued for limited government in order to maximize freedoms and free markets. Private property is an inherent God-given right. People can do whatever they want with their property so long as they don't exploit others. One of the essential characteristics of the Biblical models of government and statesmanship, as described by Bern, is that they should ensure that the implemented policies should promote the wellbeing of the population. As such, it is necessary that these policies be capable of alleviating the existing torts in the system in order to be effective in addressing social issues, such as poverty. Sometimes it is not an easy task to bring the necessary help and resources to the poor, but the workhouses in England, for example, brought specialized provision for different categories of paupers — the young, old, sick, and seniors. This movement to help the less fortunate people of the society is consonant with *mishpat,* the Hebrew word which stands for justice through government through the exercise of power. *Mishpat* goes along with the God's model of government and statesmanship. When we help the poor, we are making justice possible by following the covenant laws of God. People have rights and people have needs, the government and other private institutions could supply those needs. Being ruled by consent occurs in a covenantal system with the model of God's government and statesmanship, which could help to fulfill the spiritual and material needs of people with their obedience.

CHAPTER 3

ISSUES IN PUBLIC POLICIES

Poverty

Our nation is facing the overwhelming responsibility to create policies and programs to fight poverty at the state and national level. The root causes of poverty are the tensions between structural causes and individual causes. But foremost, poverty is a combination of economic need and behavioral malfunction of some people in need, such as orphans, the disabled, and widows. Others are victims of unfortunate and sad situations, but some of these people are considered vagrants due to their behavior. For instance, when the society is not able to support non-prescription drug users, and they are considered victims of their own choices and accused of self-inflicted poverty. Those assertions are the most common causes of poverty in American society. The fact that structural causes are digging profoundly in the hearts of people is making the things worse. What we have is a society without moral support. Instead of that, we have a society of burdens over status, labeling someone because they're poor even though they work hard. Poverty has nothing to do with dignity. There is a stigma of welfare programs and policies that must be eliminated. Welfare has been seen as a blot on a recipient's reputation; to be on welfare was to be inferior. These are terrible connotations of welfare programs' recipients who are impacted by these stigmas for a significant part of their lives. But government policies sometimes require that people be labeled indiscriminately in order to qualify for aid. A condition of eligibility is that the participants be failures. Many cases of suicide among the poor are due to being worn down by hunger and poverty. One man set himself on fire in his vegetable patch. What if we were predetermined to understand the meaning of poverty stigma using the hunger measure to capture the people's imagination? In 1985, collective generosity was showed in the "We are the World" concert to help fight hunger in Ethiopia. Moreover, the United Nations' created the Food and Agriculture Organization in 2009. The United Nations first Millennium Development Goal (MDG) institutionalized the causes of poverty and hunger to help to reduce poverty rates and hunger. Indeed the poverty lines set initially to capture the notion of poverty were based on hunger: the budget needed to buy a certain number of calories, plus some other indispensable purchases such as housing. One of the most pathetic things happening in these recent days is the suicide problem in the developing world. Governments can help limit the consequences of social and economic turbulence. Active labor-market policies, which help re-train jobless workers and ease them back into work, prevent many suicides. The debates on the current social policy are many and divided by the ideological orientation of the left and the right. But both Democrats and Republicans agree to encourage work outside of public assistance.

The Social Security Act was racially coded. Excessive government intervention leads to lower quality and higher costs in every area of welfare but mostly in healthcare. The Democrats and their ideology describe entitlements favorably, as "social insurance" earned by hard-working Americans.

One way to start thinking about antipoverty strategies is to learn about what made people poor. In February 1964, Newsweek magazine profiled nine poor households. In judging these cases, it helps to know that experts thought that the annual poverty line for a family of four would be $3,000 to $4,000 and for an individual about 11,500. Advocates class analysis without ignoring the particularities of race and gender. Includes affirmative action, paid family leaves, and public support for child care in his proposals, but his analysis pays little attention to the complexities of race and gender in liberal politics in the 1960s and 1970s. Perhaps, but this kind of assertion risks blaming feminist and minority activists for the broader left's failure — a frequently articulated but fallacious argument that does little to promote the kind of progressive politics some politicians favors, and brushes off concern about 'family values' as merely a conservative distraction. The Liberals and the leftists, shared with their conservative opponents a bedrock, and seriously constraining, commitment to extending the male-breadwinner 'family wage' to the poor. Ideas about family, as much as about capitalism, are crucial to understanding the USA's lost war on poverty. The fiscal policies of "government expending" are going to help fight unemployment, but also are perpetuating the government continuous deficit and the unemployment rates should be diminished for some cyclical economic seasons. However, the poverty problem is going to be persistent if the Government is not allowing the peoples to be industrious and proactive in the creation of their own enterprises to fight the lack of production that leads to poverty. The only way to achieve the best balance is to take out the majority of the regulations that prevent free the flow of demand and supply.

Health Care

The U.S. health care system has deeply embedded, disruptive tensions with conflicting expectations among patients, clinicians and public health, and government policymakers. The general public, patients, and voters prefer the unfettered choice of medical providers and comprehensive low-cost insurance while medical professionals wants to practice autonomy and access to the latest science and technology. Now the question is: how do we deal with these differing views about the healthcare programs in our nation?

The passing of the Patient Protection Affordable Care Act (PPACA) was an epic battle between different ideologies, the liberals' versus the conservatives' vision of public policy. The legislation was successfully implemented but we are not entirely sure about whether the legislation will be producing the intended effects. Our health system in the United States combines public and private institutions without central planning or coordination. How far could the federal government go with these health reforms? Physicians, dentists, and psychologists were charging a fee for services (FFS). This traditional system shifted during recent decades, moving away from FFS towards coordinated care systems, driven by two different, often contending, and forces: Government programs attempting to control expending and to improve quality and second the organizational consolidation and integration by insurance companies, hospitals, and physicians. That was a very intrusive movement that went to begin to restrict patient choice of hospitals, physicians, and other providers.

Inequality in access to Health Care

In 2012, there were 26 million uninsured people in the United States. Low-income working adults and young adults as well as persons living in the South and the West of the United States are more likely to be uninsured. Sixty percent of those without insurance are in families with at least one full-time worker, but whose employer does not provide insurance or who cannot afford the premiums (Marris,2018, 300). The uninsured, even if they are admitted to hospitals, receive less care, fewer tests and other procedures, and are dismissed earlier than insured persons with the same conditions. Their death rates are substantially higher. Now we're left with the question: could this be considered discrimination? Those disparities refer to unjustifiable inequalities in the receipt of health care and differences in health outcomes according to race and ethnicity, income, education, and occupation. The key debates are not only ideological debates but social debates about how to address the people's most basic needs to have a decent life, health, and education.

■ Education

Education policy is a big challenge in our nation since the American people have many disagreements over the fundamental values that guide education policies. Conservative ideology links educational achievement to individual initiatives and responsibility, suggesting that the economic and social inequalities should be attributed to differences in personal initiatives and abilities. The traditional conservative thought is in opposition to an expansion of federal involvement in education policy. Liberal ideology reflects a conviction that government has an obligation to compensate for social inequities resulting from individual differences. We have two main principles directing education policy in the United States: first, education should be free and universal. Second, education should be controlled at the local level. Thomas Jefferson purported that the system of free public education is essential for democracy.

At the end of the Second World War there was an increase in school enrollment. After the 1950s, the capital expenditures for education had either reduced or suspended. After the war, it was challenging to accommodate a dramatic increase in enrollment. The federal legislation failed to pass because it entangled two broad areas of social conflict: public education versus private sectarian education (the problem of separation of church and state) and integrated versus segregated schools (the issue of racial discrimination). In addition, interest groups divided along national versus local control lines. Liberals tended to support increased federal aid and viewed federal funding as a means of improving education quality and as a solution to inequality in educational spending.

In 1964, President Johnson adopted an approach that emphasized a range of categorical assistance programs designed to remedy specific problems, especially the educational needs of disadvantaged children. The Elementary and Secondary Education Act (ESEA) provided federal funding to local public schools to give monetary aid per child but not for the schools. The problem is that the ESEA had the long-term effect of significantly expanding the policy without a corresponding increase in federal aid. If education should be used to prepare people to have better jobs and opportunities, to grow and live a better life, why are liberals trying to push their views of government responsibility over parental guidance? The people should be responsible for their own growth and personal development. That would allow the government to be smaller, with fewer burdens and with a less expanding role. Education as a remedy for social inequality should be one of the most critical educational objectives, but it's now a political conflict.

One issue is inequality in financial resources for schools districts. These traditionally correspond to the city taxes imposed on city properties, which generate 44% of elementary and secondary school revenues. The result is a system where the local school district's tax revenues are limited by the value of the taxable property. The state governments were trying to find a reform to correct the financial disparities and to force the schools' finance reform to foster equality. According to Serrano vs. Priest (1971), under the provisions of the California constitution, education is a fundamental right that cannot be a condition of the wealth of a child's parents or neighbors. This doctrine of fiscal neutrality found that reliance on the property tax resulted in extreme financial disparities among school districts.

Another source of policy conflict is the No Child Left Behind policy (NCLB) from President Bush. This educational policy initiative was signed into law in 2002. The criticism of NCLB from the liberals is linked to the lack of federal funding for implementation across the fifty states. The conservatives tend to oppose NCLB because the government makes curricular decisions that, historically, are the domain of local districts.

Finally, another source of unresolved issues in regard to education was the concept of the charter school: a school designed to allow the creation of an independent legal entity with responsibility for delivery of education programs. These types of schools present a unique opportunity for education reform and serve as a mechanism for educational reform and innovation, but their critics see the movement as merely a modification of voucher-funded schools.

Flaws in Social Policy from the 1960s onward

The major flaws of social policy in the 60s were in the following categories:

- How much involvement and control the federal government should exert after they allocating funds to needs such as education reform, healthcare coverage, and the creation of jobs to fight poverty.

On the '60s, one of the most rewarding and influential things that happened at that moment was the Money and the Status that this money could provide, the money was buying the status on society.

- The revolution in social policy altered status relationships within poor communities.

- The status was withdrawn from the low-income, independent working family, with disastrous consequences to the quality of life of such families.

- The poor were the objects of the "affluent ambivalences" and the affluent guilt that shaped status rewards among poor's while affecting poor persons less directly.

- The larger society invalidated the "good values" in smaller communities, and the federal government explains that the riots on the '60s and civil disorder were essentially due to white racism.

- The creation of the "structural poverty" was embedded within the system and will not be eradicated by economic growth. Some welfare policies required a person to be a "failure" in order to be considered.

■ A Biblical model of Government and Statesmanship

The Bible offers a set of guidelines as well as principles that each person must follow. Additionally, history shows that the government and the church should work together. The church guides the actions of the government. However, the government in most cases, especially, when creating various policies fails to address the pertinent and rampant issues affecting the population through the implementation of effective and beneficial policies. From a Biblical perspective, a Christian statesman should be a believer, committed and directed by Biblical teachings and principles, and at the same time practice these concepts based on the love for his or her country. In the end, such a person stands out for the truth among other positive concepts of the government. In simple terms, a Christian statesman understands that his or her actions or that of the given country must go hand in hand with the teachings of the Bible. Essentially, Biblical principles require statesmen always to account for their actions, especially when creating public policies. A large part of recent public policy in this country does not seem to be in line with Biblical principles. The public policies created since 1960 contain numerous flaws, which show that the policymakers did not observe basic Biblical concepts. The Bible teaches operation of a government that administers fairness to people, basing its principles on the teachings of God. However, the presented description of the flaws in public policy shows that those responsible did not follow the teachings and the basic Biblical principles.

Our country is in jeopardy of being lost and losing our liberties with the influx of so many poor and non-educated people from many poor Latin-American and African countries. These other ethnic groups are reluctant to integrate with United States' culture and they are trying to impose their own customs. We are losing ground and failing to keep our covenant with God.

CHAPTER 4

RELIGION AND POLITICS TODAY

Evaluation of the interface of Religion and Politics Today

A movement for religious freedom has been consistently gaining force in the United States. Religious rights are among the most important things for the American citizens fostered by the Evangelical and fundamentalist churches.

In this regard, the Southern Baptist, Assemblies of God and other smaller movements are spreading the gospel and religiosity to political life with the creation of religious advocacy groups like Focus on the Family and the Christian Coalition.-- the latter being the creation of former presidential candidate and televangelist Rev. Pat Robertson.. While religiosity is more common among liberals in the United States than in other parts of the world, the majority of secularists in America are on the left of the political spectrum. The Christian right has expressed that their faith and their right to declare it has been under a strong attack by the secular left from a ban on Wal-Mart employees that greet the patrons with Merry Christmas until the display of the Ten Commandments has come under attack. Leaders on the religious rights have applied pressure on both Congress and the Republican Party platform writers to incorporate the imperatives of fundamental Christian social doctrine into policy proposals. The new Christian right has focused on the reintroduction of devotional observance in the public sector, especially in public schools. The First Amendment states that "Congress shall make no law respecting an establishment of religion, or prohibiting the free exercise thereof" but many of the values that the social conservatives and religious right define as part of the essence of the American community are religiously based. The religious right, therefore, seeks to impose conformity on these values through law and social policy, an objective that comes into conflict with the concept of the open society.

There are two distinct religious clauses in the First Amendment: the Establishment clause, which is concerned with preventing the government from promoting or aiding religion and the Free Exercise clause, which is concerned with preventing the government from use either of these clauses to its logical extreme. The Free Exercise clause may be held to violate a conception of the other clause. The accommodations interpretation of the Establishment clause is that any government activity that aids one religious sect must similarly aid all religions. This interpretation would allow the government to promote religion in general as long as one sect never appeared stronger than any other. Another interpretation of the Establishment clause refers to the wall of séparation doctrine, and speaks to the care government must exercise in collaborating or co-mingling with religion.

A recent case pertaining to this tension between two important interests involves an American non-publicly traded company, Hobby Lobby, whose owners claimed that the Free Exercise clause of the constitution and the Religious Freedom and Restoration Act protect their religious right to be exempt from including contraceptive services in health coverage for their employees . However, the government can demonstrate public interest that would justify the government burdening the Free Exercise rights.

■ The State of Competing for Political Ideologies in the Policy Arena Today

The right and the left ideologies are fighting vigorously for their beliefs on justice and for the legitimacy of altering social institutions to achieve greater equality in material condition. The courts are more able to protect the pluralistic interpretation of the First Amendment of the US Constitution, which is the legitimate coexistence of varying beliefs and points of view.

The open society, which provides for tolerance and diversity of all political, social, and religious points of view, is a philosophy that the U.S. Supreme Court has appeared increasingly more willing to side with when interpreting the constitutional rights of individuals. That idea runs counter to the moral values of groups both on the left and the right of the political spectrum. As these groups' attempt to enact their moral values as public policies, their ideas sometimes conflict with an individual's constitutional rights.

During the 1970s, the Supreme Court ruled in the case *Roe v. Wade* that the constitutional right to privacy included a woman's right to an abortion. This created a backlash which was the catalyst for a coalition between conservative Democrats and conservative Republicans. The Evangelist Jerry Falwell created the Moral Majority during the late '70s. When President Reagan came to power in 1980, he heralded a process of transformation of the American Right that had been occurring for decades. It was a change on the economic-business side from the neoclassical (free market and pro-business economics to be transformed into a neo-populist party of the right. This blue-collar Republicanism reflected the populist tradition in American history and transformed the issue focus of the American Right from a preeminent concern with the protection of the self-regulating market and the interests of the business and capitalist classes of society concerned with social issues and the protection of their view of public morality.

◼ What we have learned from past policy interventions

Religion and government demonstrate some similarities in the way they expect their various followers to obey teachings. For a relatively long time, the two have shown correlation in the way they expect their followers to maintain a productive life in the community and stay in line with leadership. However, some differences arise in the way the two approaches seek to see more people to follow their teachings. Governance works by implementing laws and policies that they expect every member of the community to follow. If any member of the population fails to comply, then there is a punishment that the offender faces. On the other hand, religion wins people's hearts through many promises that the respective sacred text or basic principles offer. The scriptures in most cases promise the various followers of the religion involved that they will get a reward out of it. Religion works by encouraging its followers to evaluate their way of life and establish a new and meaningful experience that aligns with these teachings and also helps the various individual meet their objectives. With government, the governing body works by training its people so they can follow the stated rule, relate to the constitution to evaluate their way of life and also know what may face them when they break the said law. However, from a close evaluation of the two, one can conclude that for a reasonably long time that both approaches promise liberty to their followers.

If evangelicals recalibrate their Biblically grounded message for the twenty–first century, in light of their countercultural inheritance, they as Christians are allowed to live out their faith in word and deed whether on a mission field, on a school board, on a judicial bench, in the Peace Corps. Because of the counterculture, this world is their world, and today's biblically grounded Christians do not appear to be on the verge of sequestering themselves as they did after the Scopes Trial. The other principle that helps to improve the way of life of followers of both government and religion is the acknowledgment of God as the sole source of power as well as acknowledging God as a source of all power that humankind needs to succeed. In this case, the Christians need to believe in God as the source of energy and also to trust in His providence.

In governance, policies contain the assumption that the residents under the involved government should follow the procedures set and also trust in the government to take care of vital matters such as national security. However, government policies may need further revision to allow citizens to maintain a good relationship with both government and spiritual authority. The incorporation of systems that encourage the community to obey both God and the governing body may help in improving the way of life for the people. This case would involve both the religious leaders and the authorities coming together and deciding on a sustainable approach they can apply to the existing rules to encourage the members of the community to respect government power and show their love for God.

There is also a need for the government to continue encouraging people to follow the rules and live according to the constitution. Society would benefit from an improvement in the way people relate to the government. There are ongoing benefits in a continually improving relationship between community and government. Additionally, this approach will also incorporate the government encouraging members of the community to live a fruitful life with their God. Supporting people and promising them great rewards if they continue following the rules and avoiding breaking and going against the set rules will help in improving the relationship between the involved people.

The lives of Christians are accompanied by multiple issues that aim at promoting their way of life. Politics serves as one of the problems that revolve around the lives of many Christians and may have a significant impact on their lives. To some Christians, politics and governance do not impact their lives, and they take it like any other issue. Some people give various reasons regarding their option to restrain from engaging in politics. Many nations do not force their members to participate in politics and in that regard, the Christians take this chance as an opportunity to keep away from politics and any other commitment that they feel may tarnish their beliefs. However, there are multiple reasons for Christians to be involved in politics, as their actions may help in improving their lives as well as strengthen the relationship between people and their fellow citizens. Political correctness is taking priority in the courts because judges are trying to protect the minority groups from being offended by insensitivity and hate speech. A citizen can hardly avoid politics... Although a reasonable number of Christians view politics as an earthly thing, the adoption of political leadership contributes to the success of Christians in their day-to-day activities. From the biblical narratives, God initiated the first governance after creation when He gave the first man rules to follow. God then gave humanity promises that He would deliver if people followed His will. In modern day living, humanity lives in an environment in which politics plays a role in each decision that a human makes. In that regard, Christians need to ensure that they show interest in governance to help in improving their lives. Government helps to restrain evil things in the community and promote healthy living among the people. Christians need to embrace governance as it helps to prevent evil things from happening in their community. In most cases, the government punishes evildoers, which helps in promoting healthy living among Christians. In that case, since the two bodies work with the same policies, then Christians may need to show their appreciation for politics in order to facilitate its success in bettering people's lives. The action of the government to reduce crime and other evil activities in the community may directly or indirectly influence the lives of Christians, thus they should appreciate the mode of governance.

As Christians, there is a need to love others. Loving and appreciating the government may help the Christians to love their neighbors and to do as the holy book teaches. Fulfilling Biblical teachings as well as the requirements of the government helps to strengthen the relationship between people, their fellow Citizen and God, which allows for increasing love. With increased love among the people, then there is an increased harmony which prevents the presence of evil intentions toward other people's property. Christian teachings advocate the need for Christians to show love to all around them. Christians need to appreciate government and also appreciate the various teachings by the governance. Both Christianity and political teachings in the life of a Christian helps in ensuring that the Christian not only meets the goals of their lives but also promotes a healthy growth between the Christian and the nearby society.

The above cases show the need for religious people to find ways that can help them successfully incorporate their religious beliefs and the nation's requirements to assist in improving the lives of all members of the society. Additionally, the application of both religious and constitutional teachings contributes significantly toward the wellbeing and stability of more people The End of times is not yet to come. Our hope is in our Lord that brought to us the promises of the Gospel and the statesmanship in its word.

REFERENCES

1-Bakker, F.E. Statesmanship beyond the modern state. (2016)

2-Cochran, Clarke E. "American Public Policy" Cenage Learning, (2016)

3-Fischer, Kahlib. "Biblical Principles of History and Government and Statesmanship" Liberty, University.

4-Heltzel, P. (2012). Resurrection City : A Theology of Improvisation. Grand Rapids, Michigan: Eerdmans. Retrieved from https://web.b.ebscohost.com.ezproxy.liberty. edu/ehost/ebookviewer/ebook/bmxlYmtfXzU3OTk5OF 9fQU41?sid=940b5a12-cb5c-4823-94a2-d076ca33876a@ pdc-v-sessmgr03&vid=2&format=EK&lpid=34&rid=0

5-Mansfield, Harvey C. Statesmanship and Party Government" (2012)

6-Mansfield, Harvey C. Statesmanship and Party Government: A Study of Burke and Bolingbroke, Chicago University of Chicago Press, (2013)

7-https://www.mercatus.org/search/google

8-https://socialwelfare.library.ucu.edu/eras/american-social-policy-in-the-60s-end

9-Shires, Preston. "Hippies of the Religious Right". Baylor University Press. (2007)

10-Soc315-social welfare: https://people.eou.edu/socwelf/readings/week-2/welfare-expands-in-the-1960s/

11-Stevens, Richard. American Political Thought: The Philosophic Dimension of American Statesmanship. (2017)

12-Beeghley, Leonard. "The Structure of Social Stratification in the United States", the Course Smart e-Textbook, Routledge, 2015.

13-Bern, Roger. A Biblical Model for Analysis of Issues of Law and Public Policy: With Illustrative Applications to Contracts, Antitrust, Remedies and Public Policy Issues. Regent UL Rev. 6 (1995), p. 103

14-Douglas Alexander, "Responsibility to the Poor: A Matter of Justice, Not Charity | Douglas Alexander," The Guardian, October 08, 2010, accessed November 18, 2018, https://www.theguardian.com/global-development/poverty-matters/2010/oct/08/douglas-alexander-responsibility-poor-justice.

15-Englander, David. "Poverty and poor law reform in nineteenth-century Britain, 1834-1914 from Chadwick to Booth. London, UK. Rout ledge, 2013.

16-Gass, Saul I. Decision-aiding models: validation, assessment, and related matters for policy analysis. Operations Research 31.4, 1983, p. 603-631

17-Harris, Jose. "Principles, Poor Laws and Welfare States." making Social Policy Work, 2007, p. 13-34.

18-Mattison, Edward. "Stop Making Sense: Charles Murray and the Reagan Perspective on Social Welfare Policy and the Poor." Yale Law & Policy Review 4, no. 1 (1985): 5.

19-Murray, Charles. Losing Ground, Basic Books, 2015.

20-O'Connor, Brendon. A political history of the American welfare system: when ideas have consequences, Rowman & Litterfield, 2004, p. 125

21-Aiken, Linda H., Walter Sermeus, Koen Van den Heede, Douglas M. Sloane, Reinhard Busse, Martin McKee, Luk Bruyneel et al. "Patient safety, satisfaction, and quality of hospital care: cross sectional surveys of nurses and patients in 12 countries in Europe and the United States." BMJ 344 (2012): e1717.

22-Birkland, Thomas A. An introduction to the policy process: Theories, concepts, and models of public policy making. Routledge, 2015.

23-Bowe, Richard, Stephen J. Ball, and Anne Gold. Reforming education and changing schools: Case studies in policy sociology. Routledge, 2017.

24-Chappell, M. Jahi, Hannah Wittman, Christopher M. Bacon, Bruce G. Ferguson, Luis García Barrios, Raúl García Barrios, Daniel Jaffee et al. "Food sovereignty: an alternative paradigm for poverty reduction and biodiversity conservation in Latin America." F1000Research 2 (2013).

25-Cochran, Clarke E., Lawrence C. Mayer, T. R. Carr, N. Joseph Cayer, and Mark McKenzie. American public policy: An introduction. (Cengage, 2016).

26-DeNavas-Walt, Carmen. Income, poverty, and health insurance coverage in the United States (2005). Diane Publishing, 2010.

27-DeWitt, Larry. "The development of social security in America." Soc. Sec. Bull. 70 (2010): 1.

28-Dieleman, Joseph L., Ranju Baral, Maxwell Birger, Anthony L. Bui, Anne Bulchis, Abigail Chapin, Hannah Hamavid, et al. "US spending on personal health care and public health, 1996-2013." Jama 316, no. 24 (2016): 2627-2646.

29-Draper, Theodore. American business and public policy: The politics of foreign trade. Routledge, 2017.

30-Hogan, Margaret C., Kyle J. Foreman, Mohsen Naghavi, Stephanie Y. Ahn, Mengru Wang,

31-Susanna M. Makela, Alan D. Lopez, Rafael Lozano, and Christopher JL Murray. "Maternal mortality for 181 countries, 1980–2008: a systematic analysis of progress towards Millennium Development Goal 5." The Lancet 375, no. 9726 (2010): 1609-1623.

32-John, Peter. Analyzing public policy. Routledge, 2013.

33-Marsden, Doctor Lee. For God's Sake: The Christian Right and US Foreign Policy. Zed Books Ltd., 2013.

34-Murray, Charles. "Coming apart: The state of white America, 1960-2010." Crown Forum, 2012.

35-Murray, Charles. "Losing Ground". Basic Books, 2015.

36-O'Neill, Daniel I. "11 Edmund Burke, the "Science of Man," and Statesmanship." Scientific Statesmanship, Governance and the History of Political Philosophy (2015): 174.

37-Omi, Michael, and Howard Winant. Racial formation in the United States. Routledge, 2014.

38-Peters, B. Guy. American public policy: Promise and performance. Cq Press, 2018.

39-Sabatier, Paul A., and Christopher M. Weible, eds. Theories of the policy process. Westview Press, 2014.

40-Skocpol, Theda. "Introduction." PS: Political Science & Politics49, no. 3 (2016): 433-436. Stricker, Frank. Why America Lost the War on Poverty--and how to Win it. UNC Press Books, 2011.

41-Vedung, Evert. Public policy and program evaluation. Routledge, 2017.

42-Arnsberg, Conrad M. Introducing social change: A manual for community development. P. 44, Routledge, 2017.

43-Calvin, John. Commentaries of the First Book of Moses Called Genesis. Lulu. P. 12-33, Com, 2018.

44-Cochran, Clarke E. American Public Policy: An Introduction, p. 443, Cengage, 2016.

48-Ehrenberg, John. Civil society: The critical history of an idea. P. 11-45, NYU Press, 2017.

46-Gedicks, Frederick Mark. "One Cheer for Hobby Lobby: Improbably Alternatives, Truly Strict Scrutiny, and Third-Party Employee Burdens." Harv. Women's LJ 38 (2015): 153.

47-Habermas, Jürgen. Between facts and norms: Contributions to a discourse theory of law and democracy. John Wiley & Sons, 2015.

48-Leider, Richard J. The power of purpose: Creating meaning in your life and work. P 52-79, Berrett-Koehler Publishers, 2015.

49-Lowe, Kevin M. Baptized with the Soil: Christian Agrarians and the Crusade for Rural America. Oxford University Press, 2015.

50-Murray, Charles. Losing Ground: American Social Policy, 1950-1980, Basic Books, 2015

51-Navarro-Rivera, Juhem. "Beyond Church and State: Liberalism, Race, and the Future of 56-52-Secular Political Engagement." In Humanism and the Challenge of Difference, pp. 191-214. Palgrave Macmillan, Cham, 2018.

53-Pinker, Steven. "The moral instinct." In Understanding Moral Sentiments, pp. 65-86. Routledge, 2017.

54-Rossner, S. Martin Luther (1483–1546) Wiley Online Library, 2014. Retrieved from https://onlinelibrary-wiley-com.ezproxy.liberty.edu/doi/full/10.1111/obr.12234

55-Sanders, J. Oswald. Spiritual leadership: Principles of excellence for every believer. P. 11-24 Moody Publishers, 2017.

56-Sen, Amartya. "Elements of a theory of human rights." In Justice and the Capabilities Approach, pp. 221-262. Routledge, 2017.

57-Shires, Preston. Hippies of the Religious Rights. p. 206, Baylor University Press, 2017

58-Taylor, John V. The go-between God: the Holy Spirit and the Christian mission. P 114, Wipf and Stock Publishers, 2015.

59-Tolstoy, Лев. The Kingdom of God is Within You; what is Art? P11-32, Liters, 2017.

60-Witte, John, and Joel A. Nichols. Religion and the American constitutional experiment. P45, Oxford University Press, 2016.

61-Wright, Anthony D. The Counter-Reformation: Catholic Europe and the Non-Christian World. P 33-56, Routledge, 2017.